Copyright © 2021 Clavis Publishing Inc., New York

Originally published as *Superbeesjes. De allergrootste* in Belgium and the Netherlands by Clavis Uitgeverij, 2020
English translation from the Dutch by Clavis Publishing Inc., New York

Visit us on the Web at www.clavis-publishing.com.

*Super Animals. The Largest* written by Reina Ollivier and Karel Claes,
and illustrated by Steffie Padmos

ISBN 978-1-60537-699-8

This book was printed in April 2022 at Nikara,
M. R. Štefánika 858/25, 963 01 Krupina, Slovakia.

First Edition
10 9 8 7 6 5 4 3

Clavis Publishing supports the First Amendment
and celebrates the right to read.

FSC
www.fsc.org

MIX
Paper from
responsible sources
FSC® C118365

SUPER
ANIMALS

# THE
# LARGEST

Written by **Reina Ollivier** & **Karel Claes**
Illustrated by **Steffie Padmos**

Clavis

NEW YORK

There are many ways animals can be the biggest.
Sometimes, they walk on very long legs.
Sometimes, they have an exceptionally large body.
Sometimes, they're the biggest of their own species.
Very large animals don't have many enemies.
However, they must be careful when they're young.
When they're grown, they're hard to threaten.
The only exception is man, who hunts all animals . . .
But being large isn't always easy.
Long legs can cause trouble.
And a large body needs a lot of food.
In this book, you'll encounter nine animals which are the largest.
Who will be your favorite?

# CONTENTS

# GIRAFFE

I walk gracefully across the grassy plain. With my long neck and my rangy legs, I tower high above everyone else. I don't need binoculars to see where my enemies are.

# Who am I?

**Name:** giraffe
**Class:** mammals

skin with
particular
**spot pattern**

**Legs:**
4 long, slender legs

**Size:**
males up to 19 feet
(5.7 metres) high;
females up to 16 feet
(4.8 metres) high

**Weight:**
1742 pounds (790 kilos)
to 1.36 tons

**Habitat:**
warm regions in Africa where there's
lots of grass, and trees here and there

**Food:**
twigs and leaves
(especially of the acacia tree),
fruit, seed-buds

**Speed:**
I can maintain my top speed of 35 miles per hour for a short time.
Mostly, I walk 10 miles per hour.

O                    35 mph                    60

**Enemies:**

cheetahs    leopards    lions    hyenas    crocodiles

Birds that often sit on my neck and back: **oxpeckers.** They peck the **insects** from my fur and I like that.

2 knob-like **horns** on the head; hairy for the females, bald for the males

**tail** with a long **tuft of hair** at the end

big, dark **eyes** and long **eyelashes**

**Males fight** for me. They swing their long necks and beat their heads against each other at full power. During this **neck wrestling,** they use the horns on their head as weapons.

I **eat** almost all the time and **ruminate** my food, just like cows do.

I mostly **sleep standing** and not longer than 20 minutes a day. Sometimes I have a **short nap** of one minute.

I live with my **calf** in a female **herd** of 10 to 20 animals. Some herds are larger, with males, females, and calves. I can **change herds** whenever I want to.

**Men hunt** us and eat our meat. They use our skin to make all sorts of **utensils.** They use our tails as fly swatters, or they make bracelets with it.

My height sometimes gives me trouble. When I drink from a pool, I have to spread my legs and bow my neck deeply.

In this position, enemies can easily attack me. This is why there's always an animal of the herd on the watch for danger. Fortunately, I can do without water for two to three weeks. I get sufficient liquid from my food and from dewdrops on plants.

My neck is about 6 feet (1.8 meters) long, which is longer than you are! My length enables me to eat leaves other animals can't reach. My legs are as long as my neck. I have hooves that are 12 inches (30 centimeters) in diameter. I can kick a lion to defend myself, if necessary.

I need a large heart to pump the blood through my long body. My heart weighs 24 pounds (11 kilos). That's the weight of 11 bottles of milk. Heavy, isn't it?

My tail is about 3 feet (1 meter) long and my tongue is about 21 inches (53 centimeters). I eat more than 100 pounds (45 kilos) of leaves and twigs each day. I weigh 1742 pounds (790 kilos), but males weigh up to 1.36 tons.

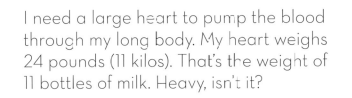

I give birth while standing. A newborn giraffe falls to the ground from a height of 5 feet (1.5 meters). At birth, a calf is already 7 feet (2 meters) high and weighs 154 pounds (70 kilos), so it can take rough handling.

# KOMODO DRAGON

I resemble a prehistoric animal and I'm the biggest lizard in the world. Hopefully you like my name, because apart from that, no one seems to find anything likeable about me. I look terrifying and a lot of people think I'm mean.

# Who am I?

**Name:** Komodo dragon
**Class:** reptiles

**Legs:**
4 strong, bent legs

long, curved,
and **sharp nails**

**Size:**
males up to 10 feet
(3 meters) long;
females up to 6 feet
(1.8 meters) long

an **agile neck**

**Weight:**
up to 330 pounds
(150 kilos)

a **broad, flat head** with
a rounded snout

**Habitat:**
vast grasslands, open forest areas,
and bush-covered hills; on the island Komodo
in Indonesia and surrounding islands

**plates** everywhere
on the body

**Food:**
carcasses (dead animals), birds,
apes, wild boars, pigs, goats,
deer, horses, water buffalos,
and . . . Komodo dragons

**Speed:**

I can make a short sprint. Then I run 12 miles per hour.

0     12 mph                                                    60

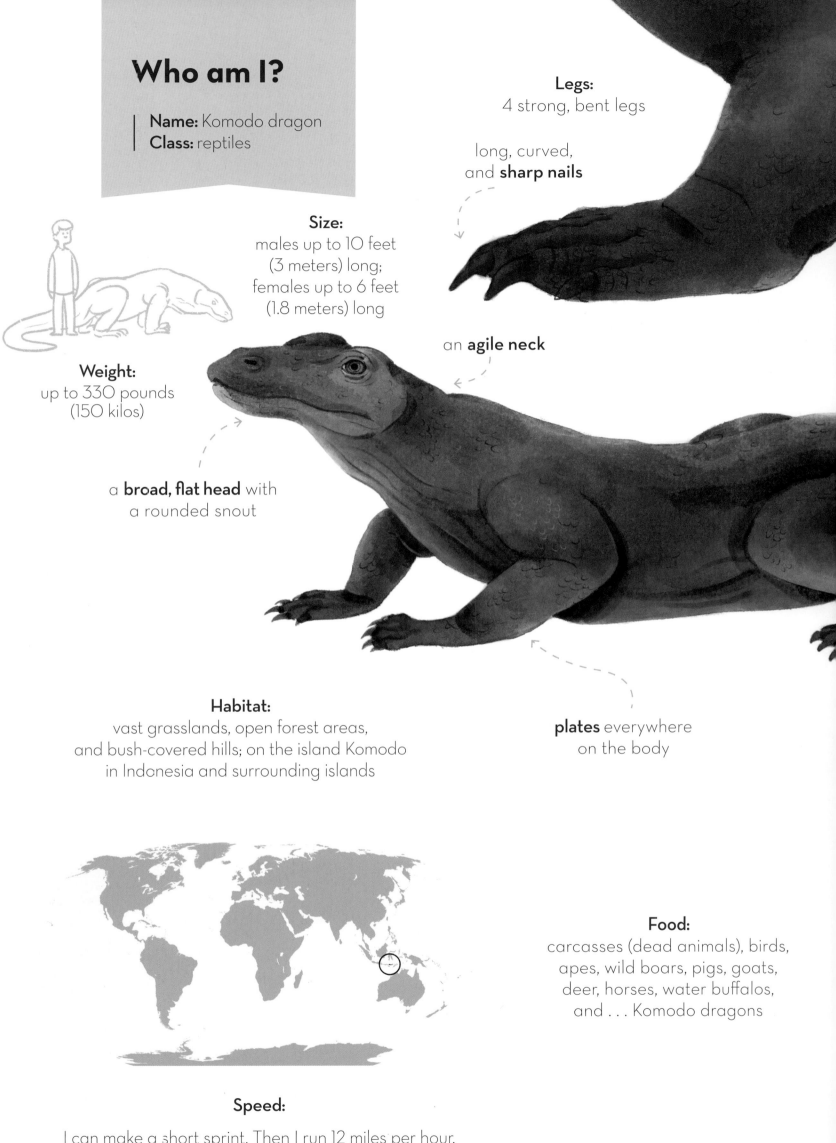

**Enemies:**
Young Komodo dragons
are eaten by:

wild boars

apes

older
Komodo dragons

Adult Komodo dragons
have no enemies.

I love to lie in the **sun** and enjoy temperatures above 95 degrees Fahrenheit with **high humidity.**

I can **climb and swim well.** Sometimes I dive in the sea and swim to another island.

I **don't hear well,** but I **see** everything that moves **hundreds of feet away.** And I have a strong sense of smell. What's special, is that I don't smell with my nose. I stick out my **tongue** and catch **fragrance particles,** which I rub against my palate. When the wind blows in the right direction, I can smell food up to **5 feet (8 kilometers)** away!

a **muscular tail,** which is as long as my body

No animal can hurt me because my thick **plates protect** me. My belly is my only weak spot, but no one can reach it.

I have 60 sharp teeth, each about an inch (2.5 centimeters) long; they're hidden in my gums, which tear open during my biting

a long, yellow **forked tongue**

We are a **vulnerable species** because we live in a **small area** in Asia. A volcanic eruption or another natural disaster might lead to our complete extinction.

I bet you've never seen such a gigantic lizard like me before. In one single meal, I eat almost as much as I weigh. And that's up to 330 pounds (150 kilos)!

With the claws of my big legs, I push my prey to the ground. I also use my long, muscular tail for hitting. When I open my enormous jaws, you can see my sharp teeth. I know exactly where to bite my victim. If it escapes, it'll still die because of the poison I have injected. I win, no matter what!

I can eat with the best of them. I have a big muzzle and a broad throat. First, I tear off a big part of my prey. Then I lift my muzzle in the air and let the lump sink into my stomach. Not just the meat, but also the skin and the bones!

When I was a young Komodo dragon, I had to watch out not to be eaten by my parents or other predators. Now that I'm an adult, no animal is stronger than me. I even dare to attack and eat human beings. I can reach the age of 30.

18

When I feel threatened, I can spit out my entire stomach content. Then I weigh far less and can run off quicker.

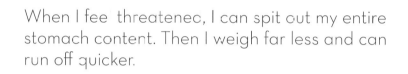

# AFRICAN ELEPHANT

The ground shakes when I approach with my heavy herd. Out of the way, please! Everything about us is amazing to look at. We have heavy legs, enormous bodies, large ears, and impressive tusks.

# Who am I?

**Name:** African elephant
(There's also an Asian
elephant, which is smaller.)
**Class:** mammals

**Legs:**
4 heavy legs

**Size:**
up to almost 13 feet (4 meters)
(shoulder height); males are
taller than females

**Weight:**
up to 7 tons
(that's 14,000 pounds!)

the legs end in **feet**
and **toes** that have
nail-like hoofs

long **trunk**
with 2 fingers

**tail** with a
**tuft of hair**
at the end

thick, wrinkled
**gray skin**

**Habitat:**
in Africa on grassy plains, stretches of forest
alongside rivers, lake regions, deserts, rain forests

**Food:**
leaves, grass, fruit, branches,
bark, and roots

**Speed:**
I can run 25 miles per hour for a short while,
but I normally walk 16 miles per hour. I can't jump
or make a sprint. What I do is more like race walking.

0          25 mph          60

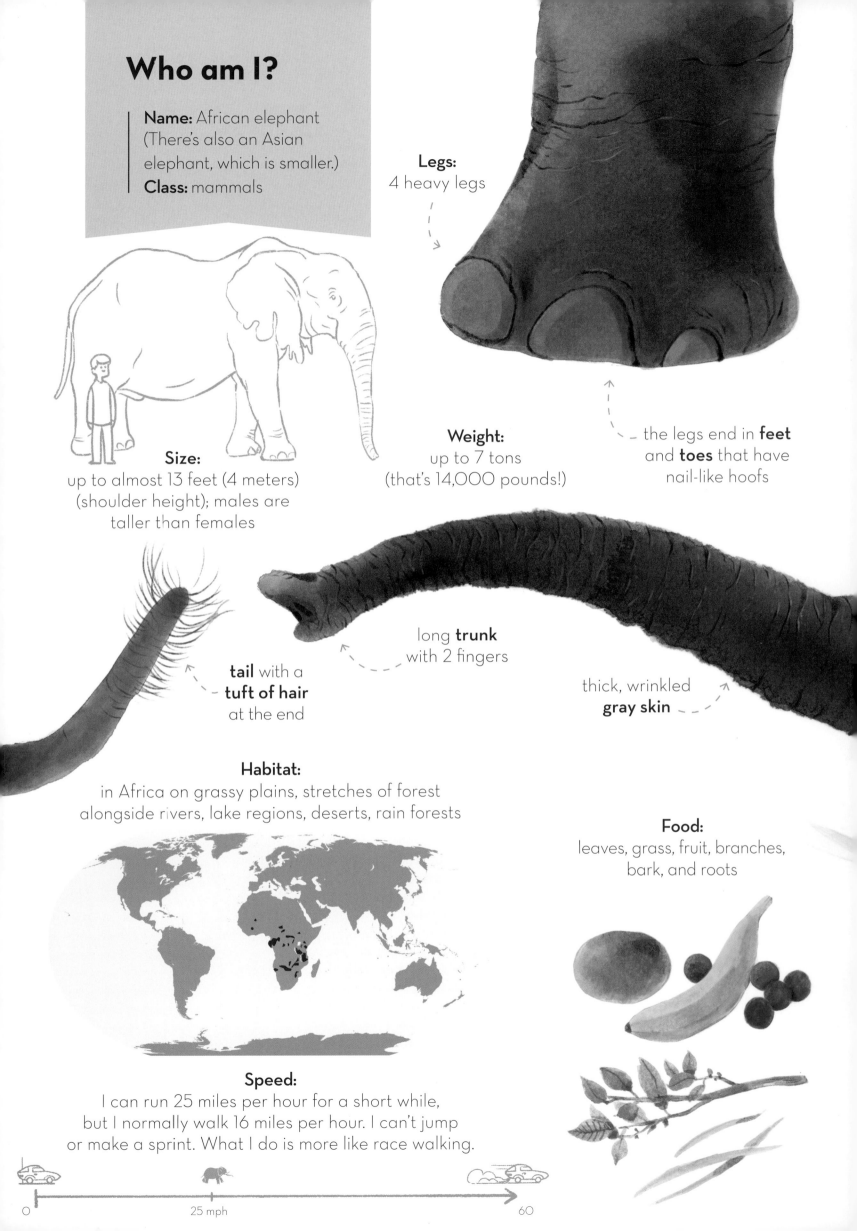

**Enemies:** Older or sick African elephants and calves are sometimes attacked by:

lions     tigers     crocodiles     hyenas     wild dogs

Adult elephants don't have enemies.

I lead a group of females and calves. We **help each other** and teach our calves how to survive. **Male calves leave the herd when they're about 14 years old.** From now on, they'll live **alone or with other males.**

We are very **smart** and have an **excellent memory.** I can remember the route to watering places and areas where there's a lot of food.

2 gigantic ivory **tusks**

**large ears** full of blood vessels to remove the heat

**Touches** are important to elephants. There are tens of thousands of little muscles in my trunk. We exchange greetings by twisting our **trunks** together. When a calf walks behind me, it grabs my tail with its trunk. I sometimes give the calves a stroke as encouragement, but also a poke or a punch with my leg.

Because of the burning **sun,** I have to **protect** my **skin.** I regularly roll in the mud. After a **water bath,** I spout sand over my back. That sand crust keeps **insects** away and makes sure that my skin doesn't dry out. With my **ears** I **fan** myself.

I **lose teeth 6 times** during my life. You do that only once or twice.

My skin is about an inch
(2.5 centimeters) thick and
I can weigh up to 7 tons. At birth,
I already weigh nearly 220 pounds
(100 kilos); not a tiny baby, right?

My nose and upper lip have grown together and have formed
a powerful, skillful trunk. I can tear trees out of the ground with it.
But my trunk can pick up small nuts as well. I can eat leaves from
trees up to 23 feet (7 meters) high. My trunk is also
a great straw and a shower. I can easily suck up
5 liters of water and spout them in my mouth
or over my back. And I can also smell and
make noise with my trunk.

With my strong ivory tusks,
I turn over the ground in search
of delicious roots. I can also fight
with them. My tusks never stop
growing. One tusk can get up to
10 feet (3 meters) long and weigh
almost 220 pounds (100 kilos).
That's quite a bit more than one
of your little teeth!

When I smell danger, I lift up my head and spread my ears open wide to appear even more impressive. If that doesn't help, I swing my head and wave my ears. I create a big cloud of dust with my legs and my trunk to protect the herd.

Hunters kill us for the ivory of our tusks, our skin, and our meat.

I eat up to 330 pounds (150 kilos) of food a day. Sometimes, our herd destroys fields and harvests.

# COLOSSAL SQUID

I live in the deep, ice-cold waters of the Antarctic. There are hardly any people who have ever seen me. I'm monstrously big, even bigger than the giant squid. I think you wouldn't like to meet me.

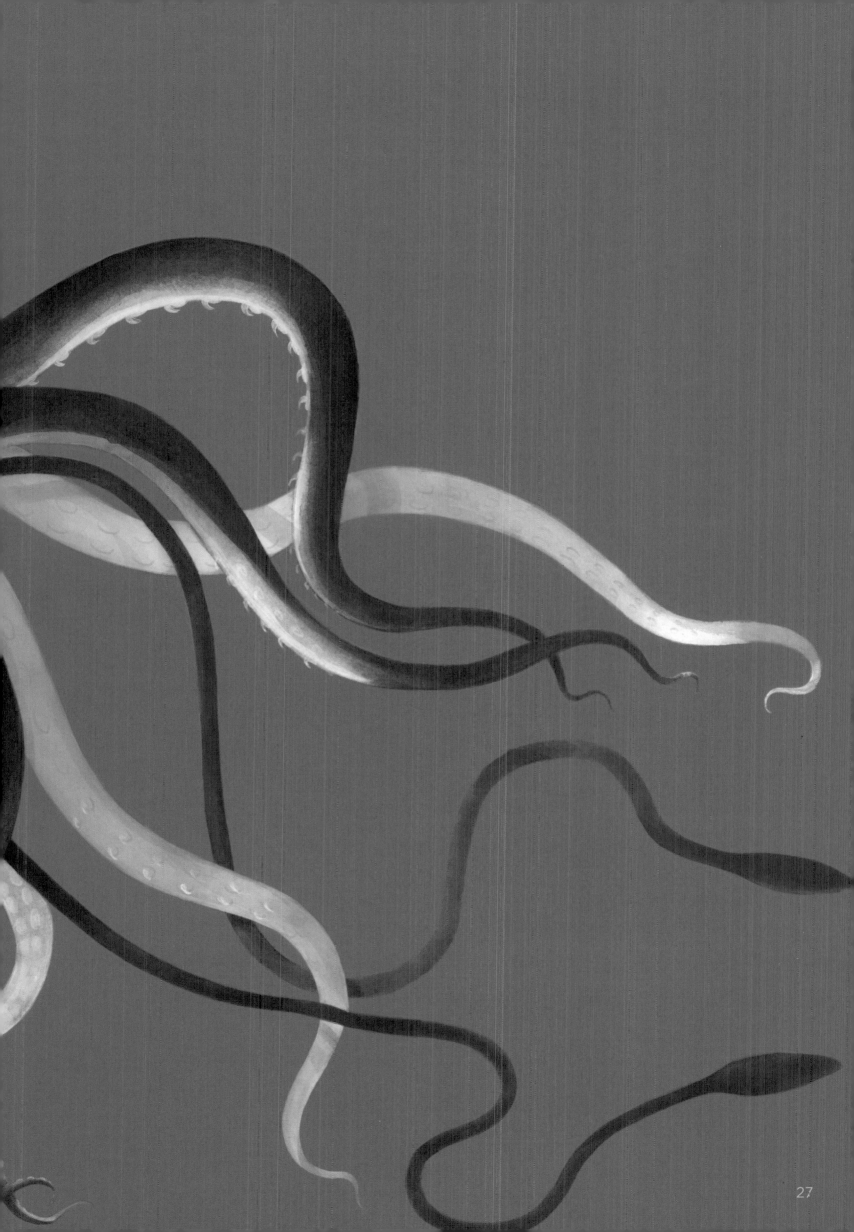

# Who am I?

**Name:** colossal squid
**Class:** cephalopods

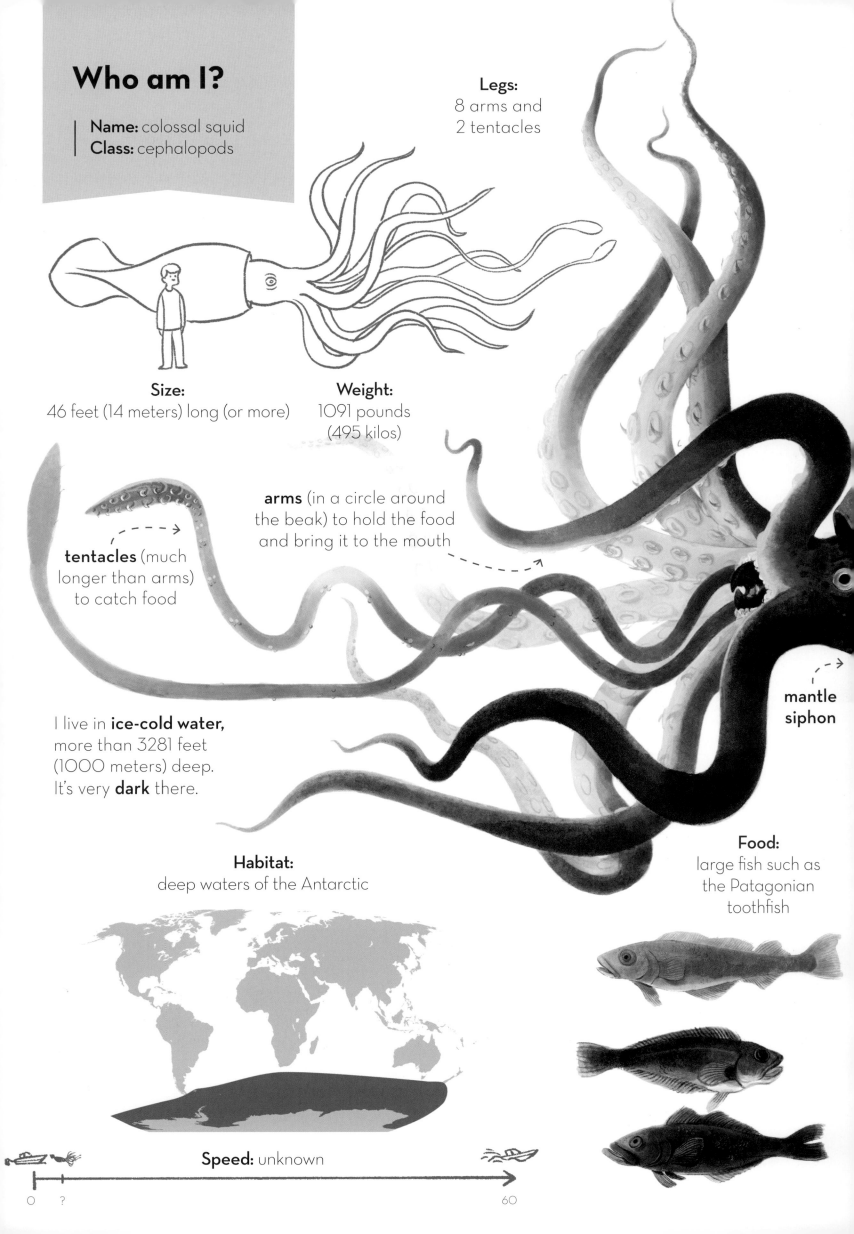

**Legs:**
8 arms and
2 tentacles

**Size:**
46 feet (14 meters) long (or more)

**Weight:**
1091 pounds
(495 kilos)

**arms** (in a circle around the beak) to hold the food and bring it to the mouth

**tentacles** (much longer than arms) to catch food

**mantle
siphon**

I live in **ice-cold water,** more than 3281 feet (1000 meters) deep. It's very **dark** there.

**Habitat:**
deep waters of the Antarctic

**Food:**
large fish such as the Patagonian toothfish

**Speed:** unknown

0    ?                                                        60

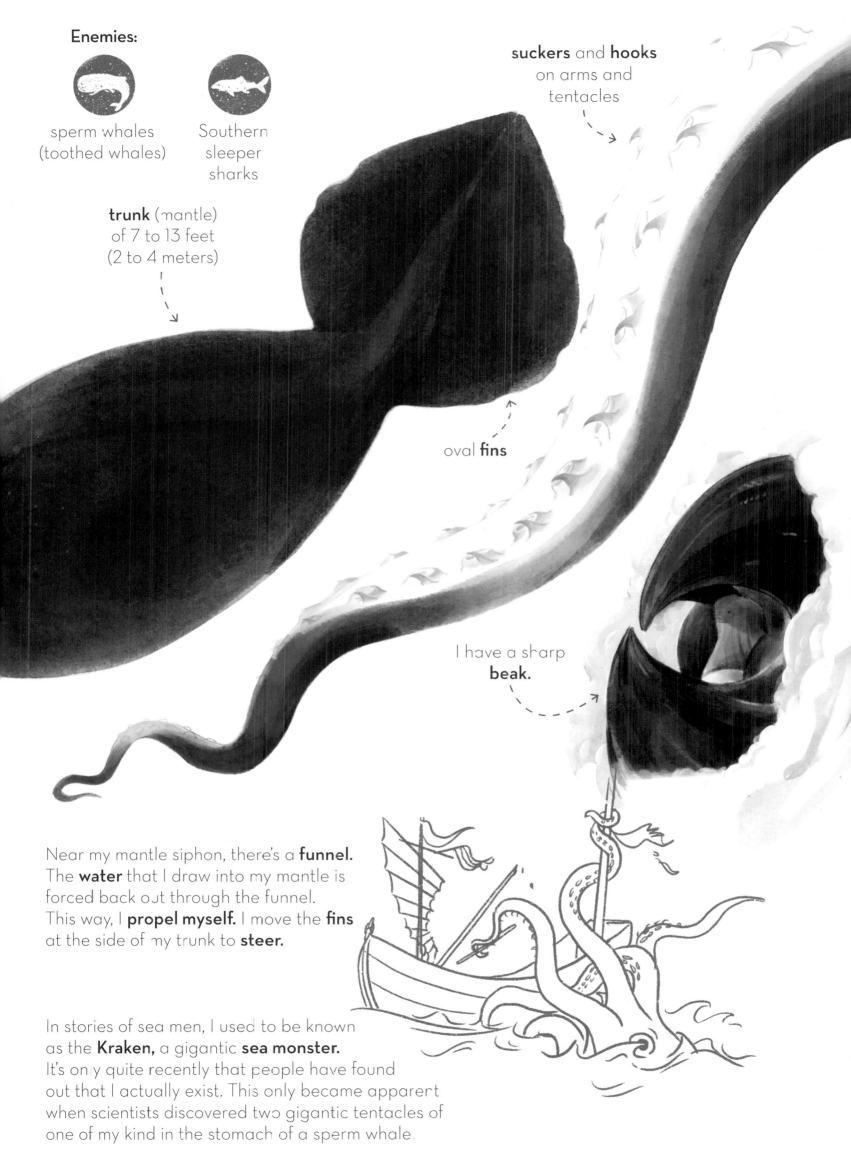

**Enemies:**

sperm whales (toothed whales)

Southern sleeper sharks

**trunk** (mantle) of 7 to 13 feet (2 to 4 meters)

**suckers** and **hooks** on arms and tentacles

oval **fins**

I have a sharp **beak.**

Near my mantle siphon, there's a **funnel.** The **water** that I draw into my mantle is forced back out through the funnel. This way, I **propel myself.** I move the **fins** at the side of my trunk to **steer.**

In stories of sea men, I used to be known as the **Kraken,** a gigantic **sea monster.** It's only quite recently that people have found out that I actually exist. This only became apparent when scientists discovered two gigantic tentacles of one of my kind in the stomach of a sperm whale.

Weighing 1091 pounds
(495 kilos), I'm an impressive
sea animal. The hooks on
my tentacles make it clear
that I'm not to be fooled with.

I have the biggest beak of all squids.
But I take my time to digest my food.
One fish of 11 pounds (5 kilos) is enough
food for 200 days!

My eyes are 12 inches (30 centimeters)
in diameter, which is as big as a wall clock.
No other animal on earth has such big eyes.

I need a lot of energy to move my enormous body. This is why I hide in places where big fish live. I can catch them easily with the sharp hooks on my tentacles.

For the time being, my ways of living remain unknown. So far, scientists have only been able to examine dead colossal squids. They can hardly observe me and my kind because we live in waters more than 3281 feet (1000 meters) deep.

# MOOSE

I'm the biggest animal of the deer family and I'm proud of it. I look very sturdy with my antlers. Unfortunately, I wear them only part of the year, from spring to November. Females don't have antlers.

# Who am I?

**Name:** moose
**Class:** mammals

**Size:** males 5 to 7 feet (1.5 to 2 meters) (shoulder height) and 8 to 9 feet (2.5 to 2.7 meters) long; females are smaller

**Weight:** 606 to 1764 pounds (275 to 800 kilos)

**antlers** in the form of sheets with a span of almost 7 feet (2 meters)

**Legs:** the 2 front legs are longer than the 2 hind legs

**short tail** of 3 to 5 inches (8 to 12 centimeters) long

overhanging **upper lip**

**dewlap** underneath the throat

**Habitat:** extensive forest area with coniferous trees or deciduous trees and water in the surroundings, in the Northern Hemisphere

**Food:** lichen, grass, leaves, branches, soft bark, water plants

**Speed:** My top speed is 35 miles per hour, but normally I walk 20 miles per hour.

0     35 mph     60

**Enemies:**

bears

wolves

pumas

men

You can find me in **cold regions** where there's a lot of snow in winter. I **can't sweat** and I have trouble when it gets warmer than 81 degrees Fahrenheit.
To **cool off,** I lie in **shallow water.** This way, I also shoo away annoying **insects,** because my tail is too short to hit them away.

I love the **twilight** and like to walk around when the evening falls or just before the sun rises.

big **ears**

**hunch** on the back
(shoulder muscles)

I prefer to live **on my own,** but in the **mating season** males and females look out for one another. When a **calf** is born, it stays **with the moose cow.** After a month, it doubles in weight.

**Each year** I have **new and larger antlers.** There's a velvety skin around them that dies off by the end of August. Because this **itches** terribly, I rub it off against a tree.

I have no **upper incisive teeth.** I clasp plants between my hardened palate and my lower incisive teeth to pull them off. And I have a **strong tongue.**

I like eating **water plants** and can easily remain completely under water for 30 seconds. I swim 6 miles per hour and can **swim** a distance of 12 miles (20 kilometers).

In my large nasal cavity, there are millions of olfactory cells. This is why I smell exceptionally well. My long ears turn in all directions to catch noises. I can detect an enemy from a long distance.

I have a lot of strength in my legs. With my front legs, I lash out at aggressors and with my hind legs, I kick them off. Thanks to my long front legs, I can easily jump over all sorts of obstacles.

I can spread out the two front toes of my hooves. My back toes give extra support. This way, I spread my heavy weight over the boggy ground or the snow. I never sink in deeply. A bit like snowshoes, you know.

A moose bull weighs up to 1764 pounds (800 kilos) and a moose cow up to 882 pounds (400 kilos). Despite our enormous size, we can walk silently through the forest. Walkers have a fright when we suddenly appear from the bushes. Colliding with a car often causes a lot of damage.

Men hunt us because they like moose meat. There's a lot of meat on an adult animal.

# BLUE WHALE

A lot of people think the elephant is the biggest animal on earth. But they don't know me yet! My tongue alone is the size of a small elephant. Do you know that even the tallest dinosaur was smaller than me?

# Who am I?

**Name:** blue whale
**Class:** mcmmals

**Size:**
males up to 89 feet (27 meters) long;
females are even bigger: up to
108 feet (33 meters) long

**Fins:**
2 pointed
pectoral fins,
a small dorsal
fin, and a broad
fluke with a notch

**Weight:**
190 tons (380,000 pounds!)

– **bluish gray color** on top with
a number of light spots,
different in every animal

flat, **broad head** with
**2 blowholes** on top

– **lighter colored lower part
of the body** with 80 to 100
**throat pleats** near the throat
and the breast; these skin folds
can expand while eating, so that
more volume can be taken in

**Habitat:**
in all oceans, preferably where the water is cold

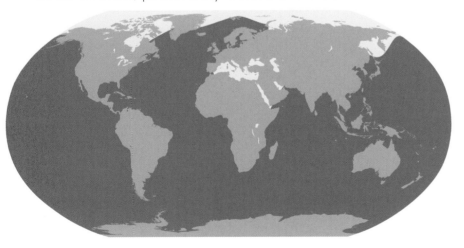

**Food:**
krill, which are tiny,
shrimp-like sea animals

**Speed:**
While eating, I swim 3 miles per hour, but otherwise
12 miles per hour. My top speed is 31 miles per hour.

0                                31 mph                                60

**Enemies:**
Calves are attacked by:

orcs            sharks

Whale hunters and
the pollution of the seas
threaten the blue whale.

From my **upper jaws,** 800 **baleen plates** hang down.
The material of these plates resembles finger nails.
A baleen plate is 3 feet (1 meter) long and continues
to grow, because it wears off at the bottom.

no teeth, but
**baleen plates**

While **feeding,** I open my mouth
very far and swallow up **loads of
water.** When I close my mouth, I push
the water out with my tongue. My **baleen
plates** function as a **sieve** through which
the water runs out, but not the **krill** I have
ingested.

I mostly **dive** up to 328 feet (100 meters) **deep.**
But because I'm a **mammal,** I have to get to
the surface from time to time to **breathe.**
Then I spout the ingested water in a 30 feet
(9 meters) high fountain through my **blowholes.**

In **summer** I live near the **Arctic** or the **Antarctic,** where
there's a lot of food. In **winter** I swim **thousands of miles** to
the equator. Then I hardly eat and live on my fat reserves.
**Calves** are **born** every two or three years **in warmer water.**

41

I'm a real heavyweight and live mostly on my own. My tongue weighs about 2 tons. My heart weighs nearly 2000 pounds (900 kilos) and is as big as a small car. My entire body weighs no less than 190 tons (380,000 pounds), which is as much as about 5000 children!

Not only am I the largest, I'm also the noisiest. I can make sounds up to 180 decibels, which is louder than the noise of an airplane engine (120 decibels). People say that whales "sing", which is what our sound resembles. This way, I talk with other blue whales, who sometimes swim hundreds of miles away. I can't see well with my small eyes, but I can hear excellently.

At birth, I already weighed more than 2 tons and I was more than 23 feet (7 meters) long. I drank almost 500 liters of milk each day and every hour, I gained 8 pounds (3.5 kilos) in weight during that time. That adds up to more than 187 pounds (85 kilos) every day!

To keep my enormous body in shape,
I have to ingest huge amounts of food.
Every day, I swallow about 3.5 tons of krill.

# OSTRICH

There's no bigger bird in the world than me. I look out over everything and turn my agile, long neck in all directions. But I can't fly! I'm too heavy for flying and my wings are too small. I can run superfast, though.

# Who am I?

**Name:** ostrich
**Class:** birds

**Legs:**
2 long, strong legs

the only bird that has **only 2 toes** on each foot

**Weight:**
up to 348 pounds
(158 kilos)

**Size:**
males up to 9 feet
(2.7 meters) high;
females are
smaller

**big eyes** and
long eyelashes

a **sharp nail** of 4 inches
(10 centimeters) long at
the end of the biggest toe

**broad beak**

fluffy, **small head**
and **long neck**

**Habitat:**
open grasslands with a few trees,
vast sandy plains in Africa

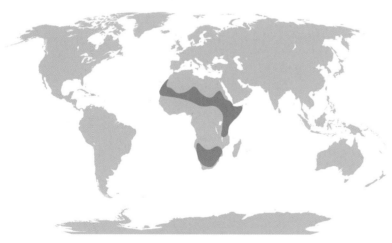

**Food:**
grass, roots, leaves, seeds, fruit,
insects, lizards, snakes, rodents.
While eating, I also swallow sand
and stones because they help
the digestion. I'm an omnivore!

**Speed:**
I can easily maintain a speed of 30 miles
per hour for one hour. But I can also sprint:
44 miles per hour!

0                    44 mph              60

**Enemies:**

lions        leopards        hyenas        wild dogs

I live in a small **family** with about **12 other ostriches.** One male and one female are the leaders. We cover **long distances** in search of **food.**

If there's a **threat,** we **run off quickly** until we're safe. No other animal can maintain such a high speed for so long.

**Females** and **young animals** are **grayish brown. Males** have short wings with **black feathers and white tips.** In the past, the beautiful feathers were used as **adornment** in knights' helmets, and later on in women's clothes.

When my enemy is still far away, I fold my legs and lie stretched out on the ground. My head and neck have about the **same color as the sand.** This way, **I don't attract** attention in the landscape. People say that I think I'm invisible when I stick my head in the sand! I have **little brains** indeed, but I'm not as stupid as that.

Sometimes I give my attacker a **solid kick.** With the nail on my strong claw, I can **even kill a lion.** I kick forward because my knee joint bends differently from human beings.

Yes, I hold a number of records. I'm the tallest, heaviest, and quickest of all birds. Well, the quickest runner anyway. Because there are birds that can fly quicker than I can run.

I also have the biggest eyes of all land animals. They're almost 2 inches (5 centimeters) in diameter. I can lock up to 2 miles (3.5 kilometers) away.

We often live together with other animals, such as antelopes, zebras, and wildebeests. While grazing, they turn over the ground so that we can find insects. We look further than they do, and they smell better than we do. When one animal senses danger, it alerts all the others.

I can jump far and high. At top speed, one step measures nearly 13 feet (4 meters). I spread my short wings to keep my balance. When necessary, I can easily jump over an obstacle of 5 feet (1.5 meters) high. Which means I could jump over you!

My eggs are about 6 inches (15 centimeters) and weigh 3 pounds (1.5 kilos), which is as much as 24 chicken eggs! All females lay their eggs in the simple earthen nest of the leader of the group. She and her partner hatch out the eggs (from 15 to more than 50) in turn.

# GALÁPAGOS TORTOISE

I'm the biggest tortoise on earth. I can't run fast, but why should I tire myself out? I wear my shelter on my back and I can hide inside whenever I want to. Enjoying the sun and crawling along leisurely are my main occupations.

# Who am I?

**Name:** Galápagos tortoise
**Class:** reptiles

**Size:**
60 inches (152 centimeters) long from head to tail

**Weight:**
551 pounds (250 kilos); males are heavier than females

**Legs:**
4 short, scaly legs

**long neck** and **powerful jaws**

hind legs with **4 claws** and front legs with 5 claws

**Habitat:**
the rocky lava grounds on the Galápagos Islands, covered with grasses, bushes, and cactuses

**Food:**
grass, leaves, plants, mosses, fruit, cactuses

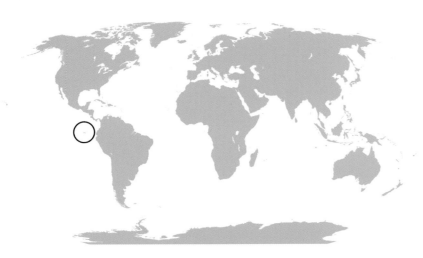

**Speed:**

0   0.2 mph                                    60

**Enemies:**

rats    cats    wild dogs

Young tortoises are eaten by rats and cats. Adult tortoises are attacked by wild dogs.

A long time ago, Spanish sea men discovered a group of islands where **gigantic tortoises** lived. They called the islands **Galápagos**, meaning **'tortoises'** in Spanish. So I live on islands that are called after me!

I have a saddle-shaped **shell.** Thanks to the large cutout around my neck, I can stretch my **neck** further. This way, I can eat plants that grow higher.

I'm best friends with the **Darwin's finches.** These birds eat the **ticks** from the folds in my skin and from my shell.

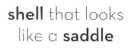

**shell** that looks like a **saddle**

I lay my **eggs in a hole** that I dig myself. I cover them with soil and flatten the ground with the underside of my shell. The warmth of the sun makes the **little tortoises** grow and they crawl **out of their egg.** I don't have to bother about them anymore.

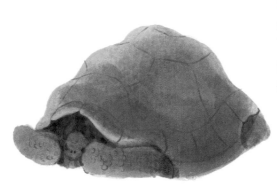

When I'm **afraid,** I hide **inside my shell.** I draw in my head, neck, and legs entirely. My shell is connected to my ribs, so I can never get out. This hard armor protects me very well.

We are gigantic and lead an easy life. We enjoy the sun and sleep almost 16 hours a day.

Every tortoise has its own rank in the group. I know my place and like fixed rules. During the warm season, I'm active in the morning and later in the day. In the hottest hours, I retreat in the shadow. During the colder season, I'm busy at noon.

I can reach the age of 150. My shell grows with me, but wears off at the edges.

'm about 3 feet (1 meter) tall and have the impressive weight of 551 pounds (250 kilos). I can live a year without eating or drinking.

Even though 'm the biggest tortoise species, my life is threatened. Horses, goats, and cows graze in my territory, which means that I find less food myself. They trample my nest. Rats eat my eggs. And human beings hunt me.

I'm not a good swimmer. But inside my shell, there are a lot of air-filled spaces. This way, I can float nicely on the water. These air chambers make my shell lighter than it seems. A completely closed shell would be too heavy for me.

# HIPPOPOTAMUS

During the day, you don't get to see a lot of my big, round body. Then I'm standing in shallow water and only my nose, ears, and eyes are visible above the surface. When it's night, I come out of the water to graze. I move slowly and look friendly, but I can be quick and very dangerous.

# Who am I?

**Name:** hippopotamus
**Class:** mammals

**Size:**
up to 13 feet (4 meters)
long; males are larger
than females

**Weight:**
nearly 4 tons

**enormous head**
with broad snout
and **mouth** that can
be **opened very far**

ivory **tusks**
that can each
weigh up to
7 pounds (3 kilos)

**Legs:**
4 short, strong legs

Each of the 4 **toes**
has a nail-like
hoof.

a **thick,**
20 inches
(50 centimeters)
**long tail**

**naked skin** which
is 2 inches
(5 centimeters)
in thickness

**Habitat:**
in Africa in shallow waters near
the coast, muddy plains, and lakes

**Food:**
all sorts of grasses

**Speed:**
On land I can reach 28 miles per hour
and in the water 5 miles per hour.

0          28 mph                    60

**Enemies:**

The calves are attacked by:

crocodiles     lions     hyenas

I live in **very warm territories.** To cool off, I stay **in the water** for about sixteen hours a day. I look for **shallow places** where I'm sufficiently submerged and where I can sleep without drowning. My **ears, eyes, and nostrils** are **on top of my head.** This way, I can listen, look, and breathe from the water. My **cutaneous glands** produce a red substance that **protects** my skin against the sun when I get out of the water.

When I was a **calf,** I could **swim,** but now I'm too heavy. I sink under water and walk across the bottom. I close my nostrils and ears and can easily stay **underwater for 5 minutes.**

People often think that I'm tame and not dangerous, which isn't true. When someone blocks my way to the **water,** I just **run** him **down.** With my **weight,** that can be **lethal.** I'm not afraid of biting a crocodile in two either.

Is there **another hippopotamus** that wants to **take** my **territory?** Then I turn my bottom towards him and treat him to a solid portion of **poop,** which I swing around with my tail. You can be sure that he'll quickly look for another place!

59

I live in a group with about 15 other hippopotamuses. But in the dry season, up to 150 hippopotamuses use the same pool! I'm the leader of our herd because I'm the tallest and strongest male. I challenge another male by yawning. In doing so, I show him my enormous tusks, which are about 20 inches (50 centimeters) long. If these don't scare him off, I start a fight.

When we go on land at night to eat, we sometimes walk up tc 6 miles (10 kilometers). I stuff myself with about 88 pounds (40 kilos) of grass. That goes smoothly with my 2 feet (0.5 meter) wide mouth. I graze with my lips and not with my tusks. Even so, this isn't an enormous amount of food for such a massive body. But then I don't spend much energy, because I don't move a lot and sleep most of the time.

I can't see well, but I don't have to at night. I smell excellently and find the grass fields by scent. When I've eaten enough, I walk back to the water. There I laze away the day until the next evening. But you can hear me, because I'm a real noise-maker. I sniff, wheeze, growl, or roar as loudly as a leaf blower (115 decibels)!